Ideas Are a Dime a Dozen

Notes on Entrepreneurial Thought Leaders
Volume 4 (2008-2009)

PersonalOpz

This book is for sale at
http://leanpub.com/ideas_are_a_dime_a_dozen

This version was published on 2014-03-21

This is a Leanpub book. Leanpub empowers authors and publishers with the Lean Publishing process. Lean Publishing is the act of publishing an in-progress ebook using lightweight tools and many iterations to get reader feedback, pivot until you have the right book and build traction once you do.

©2013 - 2014 This work is licensed under a Creative Commons Attribution-ShareAlike 3.0 Unported License. The background photo on the cover is Blue sky by Dude Pascalou (http://www.flickr.com/photos/29926644@N04/2810092063/) Creative Commons Attribution 2.0 Generic

Tweet This Book!

Please help PersonalOpz by spreading the word about this book on Twitter!

The suggested hashtag for this book is #personalopz.

Find out what other people are saying about the book by clicking on this link to search for this hashtag on Twitter:

https://twitter.com/search?q=#personalopz

Also By PersonalOpz

Passions and Other Lessons

Capital is No Longer a Constraint

Cut the Lifeboats

Start Making Dreams

Execution and Other Lessons

There Are No Rules

Thanks to Stanford University for this inspiring resource. And my family for further inspiration and support.

Contents

Preface	1
Retooling Early Stage Development	2
The Next Wave of Industry: Global Clean Tech	4
Balancing Economy, Equity, and Ecology Through Design	6
The Black Swans of Energy Invention	7
Is Innovation Withering on the Vine?	9
A Cuil Tune-up for Search Engines	11
Young at Heart: How to Be an Innovator for Life	12
13 Mistakes and 13 Brilliant Strokes	14
The Growth and Bloom of Cooliris	16
Making a Big Company Feel Small	17
A History of Venture Capital	18
Emerging Opportunities in a Post IT Marketplace	19
Innovation as the Crux of Entrepreneurship	20
What is the Next Big Thing?	21

CONTENTS

Developing the Future of Home Healthcare 23

Vision Matters 24

Building an Organization, Building a Team 26

Spotlight on Scalability 27

Under the Lid of BioFuelBox 29

The Future of Microsoft, The Future of Technology 31

Inside the Mind of a Reluctant Entrepreneur 33

Clean Tech Challenges and Solutions 34

The Art of Teaching Entrepreneurship and Innovation . . 35

Thanks for Reading 37

Preface

The director of the Stanford Technology Ventures Program, Tina Seelig, has given a couple of the talks over the years. There is one line that she uses that really speaks to me on multiple levels. "Never miss an opportunity to be fabulous."

From an entrepreneurial point of view that could mean that your product or service be polished when you launch it to the world. Or that you concentrate on your strengths and find others that are fabulous where you are weak.

However what I think that line really speaks to is your everyday life. Some ways you can be fabulous today:

- Set your alarm an hour earlier and get some exercise in.
- Make that hug last a few seconds longer when your child leaves for school.
- Get some coffee or pastries for the team when you stop for your coffee.
- Hold your tongue when somebody is rude to you. Smile back at them.
- Go the extra mile on the customer complaint.
- Polish that spreadsheet or presentation.
- Do a good deed.
- Make dinner for your family rather than getting carry out.

Those are just a few thoughts off of the top of my head. I know I'm going to try some of those out and I urge you to as well.

I wish you a fabulous 2014.

Will

Retooling Early Stage Development

Date: 2008-10-01

Speaker: Steve Blank (Serial Entrepreneur)

Link: Entrepreneurial Thought Leaders[1]

Entrepreneurship is chaotic, unpredictable, and will change from minute to minute.

Out of failure comes success.

Most entrepreneurs are focused on getting to launch and first customership.

Less than 10% of startups fail because the engineers were wrong.

Most startups, in every field other than life sciences, fail (over 90%) because they didn't find a market and customers.

If you're doing a web based company you should release often (several times a day).

Get out of your office or dorm room and test two hypotheses about your business: show that there are customers out there and that they will pay you money to solve their problem

The goal of a customer development process is to simply take the hypotheses about your business or product as is and see if there are customers and a market outside of the building.

This process puts you in continuous contact with the customers.

Great ideas are built into companies with continued contact and feedback from customers.

---

[1]http://ecorner.stanford.edu/authorMaterialInfo.html?mid=2048

Great engineers understand what customers need.

Customer creation is about how do we create demand for companies.

The people capable of changing strategy need to be the ones hearing good news and bad.

Getting feedback from customers is the most valuable thing you will do as entrepreneurs. It is not outsourceable.

Customer validation sometimes requires you to re-engineer the problem.

Until you have your first customer all of the tips and tricks that big companies do are divide by zero (they don't work).

Discover what the minimum feature set is and start with that. Do A/B testing on features.

Go for minimum feature set.

You won't know what the minimum feature set is inside of the building.

In areas where there is market and customer risk customer development, or its equivalent, will become a fundamental part of your toolkit.

Some problems (such as cleantech) are technology risk at first and then become customer development problems.

The job of a great entrepreneur is to become a domain expert–enough to understand a day in the life of their customer, buyer, and anybody else in their organizational chain.

The Next Wave of Industry: Global Clean Tech

Date: 2008-10-08

Speaker: Erik Straser (MDV)

Link: Entrepreneurial Thought Leaders[2]

The next 40% percent of people on this planet are going to achieve an American middle-class standard of living in the next 25 to 50 years.

Figure out how to find a long wave (a trend that will permeate your career for the next ten to thirty years).

Jumping on a wave as a professional will be one of the smartest things you ever do.

Think about the specific problem you're solving.

Carbon is going to become the third currency on this planet. Cost of capital, cost of barrel of oil, cost of CO_2.

One of the challenges of being an investor is knowing what you want to invest in.

Venture is more policy influenced than it has been.

The biggest markets are international.

Partnerships come in every flavor.

It is unlikely that any one technology dominates all applications.

Technology becomes very application specific.

The average U.S. car is on the road for 11 to 12 years.

---

[2]http://ecorner.stanford.edu/authorMaterialInfo.html?mid=2049

The long term goal is to take the byproducts of coal and turn them into other equally valuable products.

As a base load technology nuclear makes the most sense.

Balancing Economy, Equity, and Ecology Through Design

Date: 2008-10-15

Speaker: William McDonough (Architect and Author)

Link: Entrepreneurial Thought Leaders[3]

Commerce is the engine of change.

You can't do business with somebody very long if you're not honest.

Book: Cradle to Cradle

Being less bad is not that good.

Any business that doesn't have income doesn't thrive.

It is an executive's job to be effective and do the right thing. It is a manager's job to be efficient and do something the right way.

Are we being efficient with the right thing first rather than being efficient with the wrong thing?

Materials don't know if they're good or bad.

---

[3]http://ecorner.stanford.edu/authorMaterialInfo.html?mid=2050

The Black Swans of Energy Invention

Date: 2008-10-22

Speaker: Vinod Khosla (Khosla Ventures)

Link: Entrepreneurial Thought Leaders[4]

You can't be reasonable and do unreasonable things.

Try and fail but don't fail to try.

Almost anything you can imagine you can do. You just need to try hard enough.

Technology needs to get to relevant scale at relevant cost.

Adoption risk matters.

Separate what really matters (what is material) from what is just feel-good stuff.

You can save 10 tons of carbon a year by painting a small area of your roof white.

CCS: Carbon Capture and Storage

The only way to predict the future is to invent it.

There are positive black swans and negative black swans.

Black swans are retrospectively predictable.

Without a big problem nobody pays you to solve it.

Solve the 80%. That is where the big opportunity comes from.

Look at reality rather than stock prices.

---

[4] http://ecorner.stanford.edu/authorMaterialInfo.html?mid=2051

If you build something people want to use then rest will take care of itself.

No matter what scale you look at the power of entrepreneurship and ideas works.

Building on other people's ideas is a central component of making progress.

Don't accept conventional wisdom blindly.

Efficiency isn't cost effective or not. It depends on for what.

People who get into entrepreneurship to make money are generally not as successful as people who get into entrepreneurship because they believe in their mission.

It is the missionaries, not the mercenaries, who are really successful.

If you believe in what you're doing you'll sell your heart out. You'll convince people to join you.

There is no entrepreneurial effort that doesn't run into problems.

Generally unless you're big you don't have impact. Having a global impact means you're big in some way.

The difference between $0-$1,000,000 and $0-$1,000,000,000 is all about the attitude.

The world doesn't work from the top down.

The world works from the bottom up.

Is Innovation Withering on the Vine?

Date: 2008-10-29

Speaker: Judy Estrin (JLabs)

Link: Entrepreneurial Thought Leaders[5]

Don't take innovation for granted.

Innovation is what drives the economy.

Innovation doesn't just happen.

As we have become more short-term focused we've become more risk averse.

Innovation is about the capacity to change.

Innovation is iterative.

Talent really, really matters.

For an ecosystem to sustain life it must be in balance.

Innovation, in the end, is done by people and teams.

If you frame a question judgmentally you'll get a very different answer than if you frame a question in an open manner.

Innovators have to be critically optimistic.

Any innovative organization needs to make it okay to fail.

If it isn't okay to fail then nobody will ever try anything.

Collaboration is a very important component to innovation.

---

[5] http://ecorner.stanford.edu/authorMaterialInfo.html?mid=2052

If you have trust without questioning then you have blind faith and blind faith is not innovative.

Nurturing innovation is not like karate, it is like gardening.

No business operates in a vacuum.

We need to embrace globalization.

It is more important than ever for leaders to be collaborative and inclusive in their leadership style.

Often companies make the mistake of scaling too early.

Fail early and fail often.

A Cuil Tune-up for Search Engines

Date: 2008-11-05

Speaker: Anna Patterson (Cuil)

Link: Entrepreneurial Thought Leaders[6]

Management is really important.

Timing is luck. It is bad luck to have bad timing.

You can't get by without execution.

Stick to your vision.

One of the things you get to do as a startup is to say that we're going to start here and evolve.

---

[6] http://ecorner.stanford.edu/authorMaterialInfo.html?mid=2053

Young at Heart: How to Be an Innovator for Life

Date: 2008-11-12

Speaker: Tom Kelley (IDEO)

Link: Entrepreneurial Thought Leaders[7]

Be childlike as often as possible. Be childish as little as you can.

The surefire way to spot an American overseas is to look at their shoes.

If you can have a higher state of awareness than the people around you have then you will spot more opportunities.

Yogi Berra said, "You can observe a lot by watching."

Proust said, "The real act of discovery consists not of finding new land but in seeing with new eyes."

Sometimes the answer to, "What did we just see there?" is an opportunity.

Think like a traveler. Be an anthropologist.

Treat life as an experiment.

Be willing to fail.

Ideally you're failing forward. (You're failing in a way that has a little bit of learning attached.)

It isn't what you don't know that gets you into trouble. It is what you know for sure that ain't so.

Bring your right brain into play.

---

[7] http://ecorner.stanford.edu/authorMaterialInfo.html?mid=2054

Growing ideas takes time.

Take some time to daydream so that you can engage the tortoise mind.

Know what your muse is.

If you can blur the line between work and play...that is almost the formula for great wealth.

Be willing to look silly in front of your peers. Sometimes experimentation requires that.

Follow your passions.

Nurture, build, and reinforce your own creativity.

13 Mistakes and 13 Brilliant Strokes

Date: 2009-01-14

Speaker: Hugh Martin (Pacific Biosciences)

Link: Entrepreneurial Thought Leaders[8]

If you know you're going to leave (your job), just leave.

Get the product out.

Your board is an asset that can help you out.

You need to trust your gut.

The CEO is really, really important.

Have a V.P. of H.R. that understands the hiring process.

Never ever be afraid to go up against big, dominant players in the market.

As a CEO you get to decide the culture and style that the company will have.

Young, new venture capitalists don't want grand slam hits. They want a series of singles that allows them to build a reputation.

Over-communicate all of the time.

Don't be greedy about ownership. It is more important for the board to market the company and give you advice than how much of the company you own.

Always stay focused on your customers.

---

[8]http://ecorner.stanford.edu/authorMaterialInfo.html?mid=2106

Always be courageous. Don't be afraid to have a great idea.

Don't be afraid to take risks. Life is way too short and you should maximize it.

Resist the temptation to grasp for the brass ring.

Try to keep your ego in check.

The Growth and Bloom of Cooliris

Date: 2009-01-21

Speaker: Austin Shoemaker, Soujanya Bhumkar, Josh Schwarzapel (Cooliris)

Link: Entrepreneurial Thought Leaders[9]

It is easier to just jump in.

A business plan is a slide deck.

Time is just as big of an asset as capital is.

Every employee should have an accountable metric to look at.

Finding the best people is always the hardest.

It is easy to not realize how short the attention span is for consumers.

Respect each other and know what they're good at.

Figure out where the revenue faucet is before turning it on.

Making sure users are happy is the fundamental value of the company.

Just like you segment your market for customers you need to segment your market for competition.

---

[9]http://ecorner.stanford.edu/authorMaterialInfo.html?mid=2107

Making a Big Company Feel Small

Date: 2009-01-28

Speaker: Teresa Briggs (Deloitte)

Link: Entrepreneurial Thought Leaders[10]

They enhance shareholder value and protect shareholder value.

Auditing is an important part of our financial markets functioning properly.

Attract motivated groups of people to the edges and have them work together to improve performance.

Reward your risk takers because sometimes they are driving the most innovative ideas.

Celebrate diversity.

Mix practitioners and developers.

Doing well (by your community) allows you to do good.

The needs of men and women over time differ in the workplace.

---

[10] http://ecorner.stanford.edu/authorMaterialInfo.html?mid=2108

A History of Venture Capital

Date: 2009-02-04

Speaker: Spencer E. Ante (BusinessWeek)

Link: Entrepreneurial Thought Leaders[11]

Venture capital was created after World War Two.

Venture capital democratized a very clubby world.

A company should have its own capital then it will be insulated from events outside of its control.

Raise money when you don't need it.

Stay optimistic.

Be patient.

Creative ability knows no boundaries.

---

[11]http://ecorner.stanford.edu/authorMaterialInfo.html?mid=2109

Emerging Opportunities in a Post IT Marketplace

Date: 2009-02-11

Speaker: Tom Siebel (First Virtual Group)

Link: Entrepreneurial Thought Leaders[12]

Bells and whistles are not what make great companies.

Expect an increase in government regulation over the next decade.

Unbelievable population growth.

Moore's Law drove opportunity the last two decades.

This (population growth) is going to drive opportunity the next two decades.

If I were graduating today I would get on a boat and get off at Shanghai.

You gotta go to China.

There are big opportunities in health care.

When the polar caps melt and the oceans begin to boil it is going to present some opportunities for innovation.

Nuclear power is not a renewable source. Uranium is finite.

The data suggests drilling (for oil) isn't going to solve anything in the long run.

Energy Free Home Foundation.

---

[12]http://ecorner.stanford.edu/authorMaterialInfo.html?mid=2110

Innovation as the Crux of Entrepreneurship

Date: 2009-02-18

Speaker: John Hennessy (Stanford)

Link: Entrepreneurial Thought Leaders[13]

The biggest challenge is how do you nurture and grow innovation?

It begins with people and ends with people.

If you don't take some chances you never succeed.

Innovation starts in a fragile way. It has to have a conducive environment.

It is the job of a great university to think globally.

Innovation comes down to a lot of small discoveries.

If the universities can't work on the world's biggest problems then who will address those problems?

Your work should make a difference.

Better to start smaller and excellent and then to grow over time than to start large and compromise on quality.

Draw on the best talent because in the end that is what it is about.

Money is cheap. Really good, committed advice is really hard to find.

Compensation should directly tie to (measurable) performance.

---

[13]http://ecorner.stanford.edu/authorMaterialInfo.html?mid=2111

What is the Next Big Thing?

Date: 2009-02-25

Speaker: Tony Perkins, Tim Draper, Michael Moe (AlwaysOn)

Link: Entrepreneurial Thought Leaders[14]

There are natural cycles of job creation and job destruction.

Great entrepreneurs rise to the occasion.

With great power comes great responsibility.

Lead the charge in a new direction.

The bigger the problem, the bigger the chaos, the bigger the opportunity.

Forward thinking people look at what can be done.

Don't waste your time on a small problem. Go after a big problem. Go after something really important.

If you dedicate your life to it it might as well be something really important.

Human nature doesn't change.

There has not been anything more disruptive than the Internet.

The world changes very, very quickly.

When you start your business think five years out.

Push yourself a little further.

There is more innovation in a downturn of the economy than there is when things are going well.

---

[14]http://ecorner.stanford.edu/authorMaterialInfo.html?mid=2112

A solar panel is really a semiconductor.

All technologies have opportunities to merge with one another.

Developing the Future of Home Healthcare

Date: 2009-03-04

Speaker: Elizabeth Holmes (Theranos)

Link: Entrepreneurial Thought Leaders[15]

Building a team is the most fundamental piece.

People need to be excellent in whatever discipline you're bringing them in for.

Focus on cash flow as a vehicle for managing the business.

Paying customers driving growth is the most fundamental piece of having a successful company.

Technology is an iterative process.

Have conviction.

It is not necessarily about age.

You have to believe in yourself. You have to have the conviction in yourself to make something happen.

You have to do whatever it takes to build value.

---

[15] http://ecorner.stanford.edu/authorMaterialInfo.html?mid=2113

Vision Matters

Date: 2009-04-08

Speaker: Jensen Huang (NVidia)

Link: Entrepreneurial Thought Leaders[16]

Building a company is extraordinarily gratifying but it is also incredibly hard.

Vision matters.

Everyone has a perspective.

Just because you're a visionary doesn't mean you're a visionary about everything.

Perspective matters.

Moore's law is a law of competition.

Innovation is a rather dangerous thing.

Intellect matters.

Training matters.

Unless you have passion it is going to be extremely difficult.

You have to ask yourself what the purpose is you're building the company for.

Be honest to yourself.

If you're not reinventing yourself you're slowly dying.

You have to cannibalize your own products.

You don't set the price. The competition sets the price.

---

[16]http://ecorner.stanford.edu/authorMaterialInfo.html?mid=2212

The function of a manager is to allocate resources properly for the best return.

The competition sets the price but you decide on whether you do the project or not.

You have teach people how to take calculated risks. It is a skill.

If you want to be successful grow a tolerance for failure.

Don't ever go into business with anyone you don't deeply trust.

It is better to have a niche than to be everything to everyone.

Don't be Jack of all trades, master of none.

Equity is another way of saying "what's fair?"

Every successful thing needs to be torn down at some point.

You have to cultivate new leaders.

Ideas are a dime a dozen.

Building an Organization, Building a Team

Date: 2009-04-15

Speaker: Mari Baker (PlayFirst)

Link: Entrepreneurial Thought Leaders[17]

Stay narrow and focused.

It is a lot easier to make decisions if you have a value system.

You have to maintain credibility.

Most startups don't succeed.

Find things where you understand how they tie back to making people's lives better.

Wow your customers.

Engineers should work directly with the customers.

Focus.

Be conscious of what kind of company you want and what kind of culture you want.

You want people (employees) to always go a step farther.

Venture capitalists are you partner.

Not everybody's money is the same.

If you're pulling together people from different backgrounds you need to create a common foundation.

---

[17] http://ecorner.stanford.edu/authorMaterialInfo.html?mid=2213

Spotlight on Scalability

Date: 2009-04-22

Speaker: Sheryl Sandberg (Facebook)

Link: Entrepreneurial Thought Leaders[18]

If you're trying to be an entrepreneur or a leader at a fundamental level you're trying to have an impact.

Having impact is doing something that scales. It is beyond the one-to-one impact you can have as a person.

Leadership is finding a way to get a group of people to follow the mission with true enthusiasm.

People follow those whom they respect and trust.

Having a great vision is the basis for great leadership.

The information that you care the most about is about you and your friends.

A vision that scales is an integral part of great leadership.

Think about what the connectivity of the web (and mobile) is doing.

Distribution of words is free on the web.

When distribution became free the fundamental economics changed.

Use people's time really wisely.

There is no truth. Everything is subjective.

Be a player not a victim.

Technology will not be the constraint anymore.

---

[18]http://ecorner.stanford.edu/authorMaterialInfo.html?mid=2214

The majority of charity goes from the rich to the rich (churches, educational institutions, etc.)

People give to the things they can touch and see and feel.

Donors' Choose.

You need a long run dream and a short term plan.

There is no substitute for execution.

Where is the value in what you are delivering?

Under the Lid of BioFuelBox

Date: 2009-04-29

Speaker: Jennifer Scott Fonstad, Steve Perricone (BioFuelBox)

Link: Entrepreneurial Thought Leaders[19]

There are good V.C.'s and bad V.C.'s.

Waste is expensive to get rid of.

There are a lot of ways to skin the cat.

How you scale businesses are dramatically different.

As a startup one of the toughest things to get is credibility.

Build a strong board.

It is really hard to build companies. Things do not work the way you think they will work.

Many companies blowup because of internal fighting.

Don't attempt to start a company unless you really believe in its mission and objective.

Have fun along the way.

Trying to build a career is a misnomer. Figure out what gets you excited, gets you passionate, and gets you going in the morning.

Don't be afraid to take the leap. Don't take yourself too seriously if it doesn't quite go the way you want it.

Don't think about how things could go wrong. Think about how they could go right.

Think of life as an adventure.

---

[19] http://ecorner.stanford.edu/authorMaterialInfo.html?mid=2215

You have to be self aware of what you're good at to hire well.

People with a closed mindset tend to blame other people and don't hire well.

The Future of Microsoft, The Future of Technology

Date: 2009-05-06

Speaker: Steve Ballmer (Microsoft)

Link: Entrepreneurial Thought Leaders[20]

steveb@microsoft.com

They are always hiring. There is always a place at Microsoft for the most talented folks around.

The world has too much debt.

Microsoft and Apple were started during a recessionary period.

Most things you really need to grind on.

There is a lot of hard work to get from here to there.

Education is the one industry that never gets more efficient.

People are shaped by their personalities and experiences.

Things will only proceed in large measure at the speed of standards support.

There is rarely a really bad idea that gets funded.

Four times as much venture capital would not lead to four times as much innovation.

At the end of the day the ultimate test is if you get done what you wanted to get done.

If you have less revenue you have less to lose than the market leader does.

---

[20]http://ecorner.stanford.edu/authorMaterialInfo.html?mid=2216

You have to have a clear sense of what your core competence and strategy is.

Understand not only what your own people are doing but what is going on in academia and startups.

Learn to read a balance sheet and understand cost accounting.

Inside the Mind of a Reluctant Entrepreneur

Date: 2009-05-13

Speaker: Jeff Hawkins (Numenta)

Link: Entrepreneurial Thought Leaders[21]

Entrepreneurs are as different as there are as many of them.

If you can figure out how the brain works you can build machines that work on the same principles.

When you start a new company you can't work part time anymore.

Starting a nonprofit is just as much work as starting a for-profit business.

You have to really care about what you're doing.

Success isn't just about working hard, it is about making the right choices.

Involve people in your problem.

Worry about your passions. Worry about being successful at it and all kinds of good things will happen.

You can't worry about different circumstances.

If you're batting .300 you're doing great on product design stuff.

If you can come up with a better solution than your competitor, and do that consistently, you'll end with success.

---

[21]http://ecorner.stanford.edu/authorMaterialInfo.html?mid=2217

Clean Tech Challenges and Solutions

Date: 2009-05-20

Speaker: Steve Westly (The Westly Group)

Link: Entrepreneurial Thought Leaders[22]

There are a thousand things you can do, some of which you might not know at the time, that can make a difference.

You only have one life to spend.

Whatever you decide to do with your life—make it something big.

Don't take no for an answer.

Living in Beijing is the equivalent of smoking 52 cigarettes a day.

The average American uses seven times the energy every day than the average person in China.

We need to slow population growth.

The expectation in China is to be profitable. There is no safety net.

Always look over your shoulder to see if anybody is doing it better or different.

---

[22] http://ecorner.stanford.edu/authorMaterialInfo.html?mid=2218

The Art of Teaching Entrepreneurship and Innovation

Date: 2009-05-27

Speaker: Tina Seelig (STVP)

Link: Entrepreneurial Thought Leaders[23]

All problems are opportunities. The bigger the problem the bigger the opportunity.

You teach creativity by getting people out of their comfort zone.

Experimenting is incredibly valuable.

Often we frame problems too tightly.

You need to be able to make your own luck.

Be curious.

Being an entrepreneur isn't about turning lemons into lemonade–it is about turning lemonade into helicopters. You can make amazing things happen.

Fail fast and frequently.

If you're not failing sometimes you're not taking enough risks.

If you want more successes you're going to have to put up with more failures.

It is okay to fail as long as you learn something from it.

Put yourself in a position where you're willing to try and try again.

---

[23]http://ecorner.stanford.edu/authorMaterialInfo.html?mid=2219

Don't wait to be anointed.

When you're getting a job you're getting the keys to the building.

Success is infectious.

Never miss an opportunity to be fabulous.

Everyday you have to find a way to be fabulous.

Be extremely motivated about solving a problem.

Thanks for Reading

Thank you for reading *Ideas Are a Dime a Dozen*. If you enjoyed it you can visit the PersonalOpz blog[24] to read other tips I've accumulated on business and life. There you can also sign up for the mailing list where you'll be sent future books for free.

Please don't hesitate to email me (will@personalopz.com) with any questions or comments.

Thanks again,

Will

---

[24] http://www.personalopz.com/blog/

www.ingramcontent.com/pod-product-compliance
Lightning Source LLC
Chambersburg PA
CBHW070718180526
45167CB00004B/1525